The Bunk Bed

by Jackie Walter and Chris Borges

W

FRANKLIN WATTS
LONDON•SYDNEY

Billy and Freddie wanted

a bunk bed.

A big box came to the house.

"Oh good," said Dad.

"The bunk bed is here."

Mum got out the screws.

Billy and Freddie helped.

"I want the top bunk!"

said Billy.

"I want the bottom bunk!"

said Freddie.

Mum finished the bunk bed.

"You're on the top bunk, Billy," said Mum.

"No," said Freddie.

"I want the top bunk now."

"No," said Billy.

"I want the top bunk."

"I have a plan," said Mum.

She got a blanket

and some card.

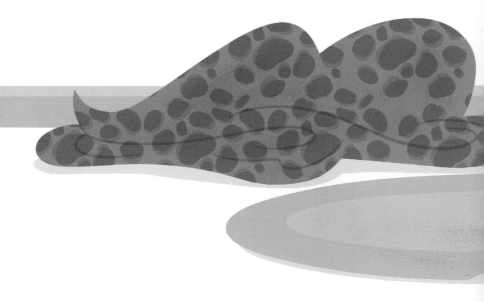

Mum put the blanket
on the bottom bunk.
She made a notice, too.

The bottom bunk was a den.

"Come and look, Freddie,"
said Billy.

11

Mum got a telescope.

She got a pirate flag, too.

Mum put the telescope
and flag on the top bunk.

The top bunk was a pirate ship.

"Come and look, Billy"

said Freddie.

"Freddie is on the bottom.

Billy is on the top," said Mum.

"Thank you, Mum!"

said Freddie and Billy.

"We like the bunk bed."

Freddie and Billy went to bed.

Freddie liked the bottom bunk.

Billy liked the top bunk.

"Can I play in the pirate ship tomorrow?" said Freddie.

"Yes," said Billy.

Story trail

Start at the beginning of the story trail. Ask your child to retell the story in their own words, pointing to each picture in turn to recall the sequence of events.

Start

Independent Reading

This series is designed to provide an opportunity for your child to read on their own. These notes are written for you to help your child choose a book and to read it independently.

In school, your child's teacher will often be using reading books which have been banded to support the process of learning to read. Use the book band colour your child is reading in school to help you make a good choice. *The Bunk Bed* is a good choice for children reading at Green Band in their classroom to read independently.

The aim of independent reading is to read this book with ease, so that your child enjoys the story and relates it to their own experiences.

About the book

Freddie and Billy really want a bunk bed for their room. But when it is made, they cannot agree on who will sleep where! Luckily, Mum has a good idea.

Before reading

Help your child to learn how to make good choices by asking: "Why did you choose this book? Why do you think you will enjoy it?" Look at the cover together and ask: "What do you think the story will be about?" Support your child to think of what they already know about the story context. Read the title aloud and ask: "What do you think the boys are doing on the cover?"

Remind your child that they can try to sound out the letters to make a word if they get stuck.

Decide together whether your child will read the story independently or read it aloud to you.

During reading

If reading aloud, support your child if they hesitate or ask for help by telling the word. Remind your child of what they know and what they can do independently.

If reading to themselves, remind your child that they can come and ask for your help if stuck.

After reading

Support comprehension by asking your child to tell you about the story. Use the story trail to encourage your child to retell the story in the right sequence, in their own words.

Help your child think about the messages in the book that go beyond the story and ask: "Why did Mum's plan work?"

Give your child a chance to respond to the story: "Did you have a favourite part? Have you ever slept in a bunk bed?"

Extending learning

Help your child understand the story structure by using the same sentence patterning and adding different elements. "Let's make up a new story about Freddie and Billy with something else they have to share. What will the boys have to share this time? What might they argue about? How could they agree to share it?"

In the classroom, your child's teacher may be teaching how verbs are changed from the present to the past tense by adding the suffix -ed. There are examples in this book that you could look at with your child: *wanted*, *helped*, *finished*, *liked*.

Ask: "What can you notice about the -ed sound at the end of these words?" Read the words aloud, and point out that the 'ed' sounds different in the range of words.

Franklin Watts
First published in Great Britain in 2017
by The Watts Publishing Group

Copyright © The Watts Publishing Group 2017

Series Editors: Jackie Hamley and Melanie Palmer
Series Advisors: Dr Sue Bodman and Glen Franklin
Series Designer: Peter Scoulding

A CIP catalogue record for this book is
available from the British Library.

ISBN 978 1 4451 5443 5 (hbk)
ISBN 978 1 4451 5444 2 (pbk)
ISBN 978 1 4451 6093 1(library ebook)

Printed in China

Franklin Watts
An imprint of
Hachette Children's Group
Part of The Watts Publishing Group
Carmelite House
50 Victoria Embankment
London EC4Y 0DZ

An Hachette UK Company
www.hachette.co.uk

www.franklinwatts.co.uk